The Black Cat

A Shocking Descent into Madness,
Guilt & the Supernatural Eyes of a
Vengeful Feline

A Modern Translation
Adapted for the Contemporary Reader

Edgar Allan Poe

Translated by Tim Zengerink

Table of Contents

Preface
Message to the Reader

Rebuilding the Greatest Library in Human History

Thousands of years ago, the Library of Alexandria was the heart of global knowledge — a sanctuary where the wisdom of every known civilization was gathered and shared freely.

And then, it was lost.

Now, we're rebuilding it — and you are invited to join us.

At the Library of Alexandria, we've set out to make every book available to every person on Earth — not just in print, but in every language, every format, and for every reader.

Here's how we do it:

- **Deluxe Print Editions at True Printing Cost** - Order any book as a high-quality paperback, elegant hardcover, or stunning boxset — and only pay what it costs to print. No markups. No middlemen.
- **Unlimited Access to the Greatest Works** - Enjoy thousands of timeless classics — from Plato to Shakespeare to Tolstoy — in beautiful, modern eBook and audiobook editions. Read and listen without limits — for every reader, everywhere.
- **Modern Translations for Every Language & Dialect** - We're reimagining the classics in clear, accessible language — and translating them into every dialect imaginable. Everyone deserves to understand humanity's greatest ideas.

When you visit **LibraryofAlexandria.com**, you're not just accessing books — you're joining a global movement to restore, preserve, and share the wisdom of civilization.

Join us today at LibraryofAlexandria.com

Together, we'll ensure the light of human wisdom never fades again.

With gratitude,

The Modern Library of Alexandria Team

Visit:
www.libraryofalexandria.com
Or scan the code below:

Introduction

The Psychology of Guilt and Madness in Poe's Darkest Tale

Among Edgar Allan Poe's many masterful explorations of human darkness, *The Black Cat* (first published in 1843 in *The Saturday Evening Post*) remains one of his most psychologically penetrating and haunting works. While it shares thematic similarities with Poe's other celebrated tales of guilt and murder—most notably *The Tell-Tale Heart*—*The Black Cat* delves even deeper into the fractured psyche of its narrator, charting a terrifying descent into alcoholism, cruelty, and madness. At once a story of psychological horror and supernatural suggestion, it presents the reader with a disturbing meditation on human depravity, guilt's corrosive power, and the blurred boundary between reality and hallucination.

Told in the first person by an unnamed narrator, *The Black Cat* recounts a series of increasingly violent acts perpetrated against the narrator's once-beloved pets and his wife. Initially a man of gentle and affectionate disposition, the narrator becomes consumed by alcohol and irrational anger, leading him to commit unspeakable acts. The turning point arrives when he mutilates his favorite pet, a black cat named Pluto, and later hangs the animal in a fit of drunken rage. This horrifying act, far from quelling his rage, sets in motion a series of events that culminate in the murder of his wife and his eventual downfall.

The narrative is framed as a confession, written by the narrator on the eve of his execution. This structure lends the story a sense of immediacy and fatalism; we know from the outset that the narrator's actions have led to his doom, and the tension arises from watching his inexorable slide toward self-destruction. Unlike traditional Gothic villains, who may be motivated by grand ambitions or supernatural forces, Poe's narrator is an ordinary man undone by his own moral weakness and capacity for violence. His story is not just a tale of horror but also a chilling psychological case study, revealing how guilt and self-loathing can distort perception and reason.

Central to the horror of *The Black Cat* is its ambiguous interplay between the psychological and the supernatural. While the story can be read as a straightforward account of madness and crime, it also contains elements that suggest supernatural retribution. The second black cat, nearly identical to Pluto but with a mysterious white mark on its chest that gradually takes the shape of a gallows, seems to embody the narrator's guilt and fear of punishment. Whether this cat is a supernatural agent of vengeance or a hallucination born of the narrator's tormented mind is left deliberately unclear, and it is this ambiguity that makes the story so unsettling. Poe masterfully leaves the reader to decide whether the events are the product of madness, fate, or some darker cosmic justice.

Themes of Cruelty, Alcoholism, and the Corruption of the Soul

One of the most prominent themes in *The Black Cat* is the destructive influence of alcohol. Poe himself struggled with alcoholism throughout his life, and this personal experience lends authenticity and emotional weight to his depiction of the narrator's moral decline. At the beginning of the story, the narrator is a man who loves animals and is deeply compassionate. However, as he succumbs to the influence of alcohol, his character transforms into one marked by cruelty and irrational violence. His treatment of Pluto is emblematic of this transformation, as the cat becomes the first victim of his drunken rage.

The story suggests that alcohol not only fuels the narrator's violent impulses but also erodes his moral compass and capacity for empathy. His growing cruelty toward the animals and his wife is accompanied by a disturbing sense of detachment, as though he is both aware of his actions and powerless to stop them. This duality—between awareness and compulsion—intensifies the horror of the narrative, as the narrator becomes a prisoner of his own degraded impulses.

Cruelty, particularly toward animals, serves as both a theme and a moral indicator in *The Black Cat*. Poe's choice of a cat as the central victim is significant. Cats, often associated with mystery, witchcraft, and superstition, carry symbolic weight in the story. The black cat, with its traditional associations with bad luck and the supernatural, becomes both a literal victim and a symbol of the narrator's own corrupted soul. His violent acts against the cat reflect not only his descent into moral darkness but also his growing alienation from his own humanity.

Guilt is another central theme that drives the narrative forward. After killing Pluto, the narrator begins to experience a gnawing sense of remorse, which manifests in strange and terrifying ways. The appearance of the second black cat, which eerily resembles Pluto, can be interpreted as a physical embodiment of this guilt. Its presence torments the narrator, serving as a constant reminder of his crime and an omen of his ultimate punishment. The white mark on the cat's chest, resembling a gallows, further reinforces this association, symbolizing the inescapable judgment that awaits him.

The climax of the story—when the narrator kills his wife and hides her body behind a wall—underscores the destructive power of unchecked guilt and madness. His initial confidence in having concealed the crime is shattered when the police, guided by the eerie howling of the second cat, uncover the body. This moment of revelation is both shocking and inevitable, as the narrator's attempt to evade justice is undone by the very creature that symbolizes his guilt. In this way, *The Black Cat* can be seen as a cautionary tale about the consequences of moral corruption, cruelty, and self-deception.

Poe's Narrative Technique and the Reader's Experience

Poe's mastery of narrative structure and psychological depth is on full display in *The Black Cat*. By employing a first-person confession, he immerses the reader in the narrator's mind, allowing us to witness his unraveling in real time. This technique creates a sense of intimacy and complicity, as though we are not merely reading a story but listening to a condemned man unburden his soul. The narrator's tone, which shifts between rational explanation and feverish justification, reflects his fractured mental state and keeps the reader on edge, unsure of how much of the narrative can be trusted.

The story's language is both precise and evocative, filled with imagery that heightens the sense of dread. Poe's descriptions of the narrator's violent acts are chilling not because they are overly graphic but because they are delivered with a cold detachment that underscores the narrator's moral decay. At the same time, Poe's use of symbolism—particularly the recurring imagery of eyes, darkness, and the gallows-shaped mark—adds layers of meaning to the narrative, inviting readers to interpret the story on multiple levels.

Poe's handling of suspense in *The Black Cat* is particularly masterful. From the moment the narrator harms Pluto, the narrative is driven by a growing sense of inevitability. Each act of violence escalates the tension, and the appearance of the second cat introduces a supernatural or psychological element that deepens the sense of foreboding. By the time the narrator kills his wife, the reader senses that his downfall is certain, yet the final scene—when the cat's howling reveals the hidden corpse—is still shocking in its execution.

The enduring power of *The Black Cat* lies in its exploration of universal fears and moral truths. It is a story about the darkness that can reside within anyone, about how guilt and self-destructive impulses can consume a person from within. It is also a meditation on the idea of justice— whether divine, supernatural, or psychological. The narrator's fate, sealed by the very creature he sought to destroy, suggests that guilt has a way of manifesting itself, of demanding reckoning, no matter how deeply one tries to bury it.

For modern readers, *The Black Cat* remains as relevant and unsettling as when it was first published. Its themes of cruelty, addiction, guilt, and moral collapse continue to resonate, while its narrative style and psychological complexity make it a timeless masterpiece of horror literature. As you prepare to read this story, consider the layers of meaning beneath its surface narrative. Notice how

Poe uses the cat not only as a character but as a symbol of guilt, revenge, and the narrator's own fractured psyche. Pay attention to the shifts in tone and language, which reflect the narrator's gradual descent into madness. And above all, allow yourself to experience the unsettling blend of psychological realism and supernatural suggestion that makes The Black Cat one of Poe's most unforgettable works.

The Black Cat

For the most bizarre, yet most ordinary story I am about to write, I neither expect nor ask for belief. I would indeed be insane to expect it, in a situation where my own senses reject what they witnessed. Yet I am not insane—and I am certainly not dreaming. But tomorrow I die, and today I want to unburden my soul. My immediate goal is to present to the world, clearly, briefly, and without commentary, a series of simple household events. In their aftermath, these events have terrified—have tortured—have destroyed me. Yet I will not try to explain them. To me, they have shown little but horror—to many they will seem less terrible than strange. In the future, perhaps, some mind may be found that will reduce my nightmare to the ordinary—some mind more calm, more logical, and far less emotional than my own, which will see, in the circumstances I describe with dread, nothing more than a normal sequence of very natural causes and effects.

From childhood, I was known for being gentle and kind-hearted. My compassionate nature was so obvious that my friends often teased me about it. I had a particular love for animals, and my parents spoiled me with many different pets. I spent most of my time with these creatures and felt happiest when I was feeding them and showing them affection. This trait became stronger as I grew older, and as an adult, it became one of my greatest joys. For anyone who has loved a loyal and intelligent dog, I hardly need to explain the kind of deep satisfaction this brings. There's something about the pure, selfless love of an animal that touches the heart of someone who has often experienced the shallow friendships and fragile loyalty that humans offer.

I got married at a young age and was delighted to discover that my wife had a temperament that matched well with mine. When she noticed how much I loved household pets, she made every effort to get us the most pleasant kinds of animals. We kept birds, goldfish, a beautiful dog, rabbits, a small monkey, and a cat.

This cat was an exceptionally large and beautiful creature, completely black, and intelligent to an amazing extent. When discussing his cleverness, my wife, who deep down had a touch of superstitious belief, often referenced the old folk belief that considered all black cats to be witches in disguise. She was never actually serious about this idea—and I only bring up this detail because it happens to come to mind right now.

Pluto—that was the cat's name—was my favorite pet and companion. I was the only one who fed him, and he followed me everywhere I went around the house. It was actually hard for me to stop him from coming with me when I walked through the streets.

Our friendship continued in this way for several years, during which my overall mood and personality—through the influence of my drinking problem—had (I'm ashamed to admit) undergone a complete change for the worse. Day by day, I became more sullen, more easily angered, and more careless about other people's feelings. I allowed myself to speak harshly to my wife. Eventually, I even physically hurt her. My pets, naturally, felt the shift in my behavior. I didn't just ignore them—I mistreated them. However, I still cared enough about Pluto to stop myself from abusing him, unlike the rabbits, monkey, or even the dog, which I had no problem mistreating whenever they happened to cross my path, whether by chance or out of affection. But my condition worsened—for what illness compares to alcoholism!—and eventually even Pluto, who was getting older and therefore somewhat cranky, began to suffer from my bad temper.

One night, coming home heavily drunk from one of my usual places around town, I thought the cat was avoiding me. I grabbed him, and in his terror at my violent behavior, he bit my hand and left a small wound. The rage of a demon immediately took control of me. I no longer recognized myself. My true soul seemed to suddenly leave my body, and a wickedness worse than any devil's, fed by alcohol, coursed through every part of my being. I pulled a penknife from my vest pocket, opened it, grabbed the poor animal by the throat, and intentionally cut out one of its eyes! I feel shame, I burn with guilt, I tremble with horror as I write about this terrible act.

When my rational thinking came back in the morning—after I had slept away the effects of the night's drinking—I felt a mixture of horror and guilt for the crime I had committed; but this feeling was weak and uncertain at best, and my soul remained unchanged. I threw myself back into excessive behavior, and quickly drowned all memory of what I had done in alcohol.

In the meantime the cat slowly recovered. The socket of the lost eye presented, it is true, a frightful appearance, but he no longer appeared to suffer any pain. He went about the house as usual, but, as might be expected, fled in extreme terror at my approach. I had so much of my old heart left, as to be at first grieved by this evident dislike on the part of a creature which had once so loved me. But this feeling soon gave place to irritation. And then came, as if to my final and irrevocable overthrow, the spirit of

PERVERSENESS. Of this spirit philosophy takes no account. Yet I am not more sure that my soul lives, than I am that perverseness is one of the primitive impulses of the human heart—one of the indivisible primary faculties, or sentiments, which give direction to the character of Man. Who has not, a hundred times, found himself committing a vile or a silly action, for no other reason than because he knows he should not? Have we not a perpetual inclination, in the teeth of our best judgment, to violate that which is Law, merely because we understand it to be such? This spirit of perverseness, I say, came to my final overthrow. It was this unfathomable longing of the soul to vex itself—to offer violence to its own nature—to do wrong for the wrong's sake only—that urged me to continue and finally to consummate the injury I had inflicted upon the unoffending brute. One morning, in cool blood, I slipped a noose about its neck and hung it to the limb of a tree;—hung it with the tears streaming from my eyes, and with the bitterest remorse at my heart;—hung it because I knew that it had loved me, and because I felt it had given me no reason of offence;—hung it because I knew that in so doing I was committing a sin—a deadly sin that would so jeopardize my immortal soul as to place it—if such a thing were possible—even beyond the reach of the infinite mercy of the Most Merciful and Most Terrible God.

On the night after this terrible act was committed, I was awakened from sleep by someone shouting "Fire!" The curtains around my bed were burning. The entire house was engulfed in flames. My wife, a servant, and I barely managed to escape from the fire. Everything was destroyed. All of my possessions were consumed, and from that moment on, I gave myself over to despair.

I am beyond the weakness of trying to establish a sequence of cause and effect between the disaster and the atrocity. However, I am describing a chain of facts—and I don't want to leave even a possible connection incomplete. On the day following the fire, I visited the ruins. The walls, with one exception, had collapsed. This exception was a compartment wall, not very thick, which stood about the middle of the house, and against which the head of my bed had rested. The plaster had here, to a great extent, withstood the fire's effects—a fact which I attributed to its having been recently applied. Around this wall a dense crowd had gathered, and many people seemed to be examining a particular section of it with very careful and intense attention. The words "strange!" "unusual!" and other similar expressions aroused my curiosity. I approached and saw, as if carved in bas relief upon the white surface, the figure of a gigantic cat. The impression was rendered with truly remarkable accuracy. There was a rope around the animal's neck.

When I first saw this ghostly image—because I could hardly think of it as anything else—I was filled with both amazement and fear. But eventually, logical thinking helped me understand what had happened. I recalled that the cat had been hanged in a garden next to the house. When the fire alarm sounded, this garden quickly filled with people—and one of them must have cut the animal down from the tree and hurled it through an open window into my room. This was probably done to wake me up from my sleep. When the other walls collapsed, they pressed the victim of my cruelty into the newly applied plaster; the lime in the plaster, combined with the flames and the ammonia from the dead body, had created the image I was now looking at.

Although I easily explained to my logical mind, if not completely to my conscience, the shocking event I just described, it still made a profound impact on my imagination. For months I couldn't free myself from the ghost-like image of the cat; and during this time, a feeling that resembled remorse, though it wasn't quite that, returned to my soul. I even went as far as to feel sorry about losing the animal, and I began searching around me, in the wretched places I now regularly visited, for another pet of the same kind and with a somewhat similar appearance to replace it.

One night as I sat there, half-dazed, in a tavern of the worst kind, something black suddenly caught my eye. It was resting on top of one of the enormous barrels of gin or rum that made up most of the room's furnishings. I had been staring steadily at the top of this barrel for several minutes, and what surprised me now was that I hadn't noticed the object there sooner. I walked over to it and reached out to touch it with my hand. It was a black cat—a very large one—just as big as Pluto, and it looked exactly like him in every way except for one difference. Pluto didn't have a single white hair anywhere on his body, but this cat had a large, though irregularly shaped patch of white fur that covered almost his entire chest. The moment I touched him, he stood up right away, purred loudly, rubbed against my hand, and seemed thrilled by my attention. This was exactly the kind of creature I had been looking for. I immediately offered to buy it from the tavern owner, but the man claimed no ownership of it—he knew nothing about it—had never laid eyes on it before.

I kept petting the cat, and when I got ready to head home, the animal showed that it wanted to come with me. I let it follow along, stopping now and then to give it a pat as we walked. Once we arrived at the house, it made itself completely at home right away and quickly became my wife's beloved companion.

As for me, I quickly began to feel a growing dislike for the animal. This was completely opposite to what I had expected, but for reasons I couldn't understand, its obvious affection for me actually repulsed and irritated me. Slowly, these feelings of revulsion and irritation grew into bitter hatred. I started avoiding the creature, held back from physically harming it only by a sense of shame and the memory of my previous act of cruelty. For several weeks, I didn't hit it or mistreat it violently in any other way, but little by little—very gradually—I began to regard it with unspeakable disgust, and I would quietly escape from its repulsive presence as if fleeing from the breath of plague.

What certainly increased my hatred of the animal was finding out, the morning after I brought it home, that like Pluto, it too had lost one of its eyes. This detail, however, only made my wife love it more, since she possessed, to a remarkable degree, that compassionate nature which had once been my defining characteristic and the foundation of many of my most innocent and genuine joys.

Despite my growing hatred for this cat, it seemed to become even more attached to me. It followed me around with a persistence that would be hard for anyone to understand. Whenever I sat down, it would crouch under my chair or jump onto my lap, smothering me with its disgusting affection. When I got up to walk, it would weave between my feet and nearly trip me, or dig its long, sharp claws into my clothing and climb up to my chest. During these moments, even though I desperately wanted to kill it with a single strike, I held myself back—partly because I remembered my previous crime, but mainly—let me admit this right now—because I was absolutely terrified of the creature.

This fear wasn't exactly a fear of physical harm—yet I would struggle to describe it any other way. I'm almost embarrassed to admit—yes, even here in this criminal's cell, I'm almost embarrassed to admit—that the terror and horror this animal filled me with had been intensified by one of the most absurd fantasies anyone could imagine. My wife had pointed out to me, several times, the shape of the white hair marking I've mentioned, which was the only visible difference between this strange creature and the one I had killed. The reader will recall that this mark, though large, had originally been very unclear; but gradually—so gradually it was almost unnoticeable, and for a long time my mind fought to dismiss it as imagination—it had eventually taken on a sharp and definite outline. It now represented something that makes me tremble to mention—and because of this, more than anything else, I despised and feared the creature and would have gotten rid of the monster if I had the courage—it was now, I tell you, the image of something horrible—something ghastly—the GALLOWS!—oh, that sorrowful and terrible instrument of Horror and Crime—of Suffering and Death!

Now I was truly miserable beyond ordinary human suffering. A wild animal—whose companion I had scornfully killed—a wild animal was bringing about such unbearable anguish for me, a man created in the image of God! Unfortunately, I no longer experienced the comfort of rest during either day or night! During the day, the creature never left me alone for a single moment, and at night I woke up every hour from terrifying nightmares to discover the animal's warm breath on my face, and its enormous weight—like a living nightmare I couldn't escape—pressing down on my chest forever!

Under the weight of such torment, the weak traces of goodness left in me gave way. Dark thoughts became my only companions—the blackest and most wicked of thoughts. My naturally moody disposition grew into hatred for everything and everyone; while my long-suffering wife, sadly, bore the brunt of the sudden, frequent, and uncontrollable fits of rage that I now recklessly gave in to, enduring them with the most patience and suffering the most from them.

One day she came with me on a household task down to the cellar of the old building that our financial struggles forced us to live in. The cat followed me down the narrow stairs and nearly sent me tumbling forward, driving me into a furious rage. I grabbed an axe, and in my anger, I forgot the childlike fear that had always held me back before. I swung at the animal with a blow that certainly would have killed it instantly if it had landed where I intended. But my wife's hand stopped the blow. Her interference pushed me into a rage that was more than demonic, so I pulled my arm away from her grip and drove the axe into her skull. She collapsed dead on the spot without making a sound.

After completing this terrible murder, I immediately began the deliberate task of hiding the body. I realized I couldn't take it out of the house, whether during the day or at night, without risking detection by the neighbors. Numerous plans crossed my mind. At one point, I considered chopping the corpse into small pieces and burning them completely. Then I thought about digging a grave in the cellar floor. I also contemplated throwing it down the well in the backyard or packing it in a crate like regular goods, making the proper arrangements to have a carrier remove it from the house. Eventually, I came up with what seemed like a much better solution than any of these options. I decided to seal it behind a wall in the cellar, just as medieval monks were known to have done with their victims.

The cellar was perfectly suited for this purpose. The walls were built with loose construction and had recently been covered with rough plaster that the humid air had kept from properly setting. Additionally, one wall featured a bulge created by a blocked-off chimney or fireplace that had been sealed and designed to match the rest of the cellar. I felt confident I could easily remove the bricks from this spot, place the body inside, and rebuild the wall exactly as it was before, ensuring no one would notice anything unusual. My calculations proved correct. Using a crowbar, I quickly removed the bricks and carefully positioned the body against the inner wall, holding it in place while I rebuilt the entire structure to its original appearance with minimal effort. After obtaining mortar, sand, and hair with the utmost care, I mixed plaster that perfectly matched the existing material and meticulously covered the new brickwork. Once finished, I was completely satisfied with the result. The wall showed absolutely no signs of disturbance. I gathered every piece of debris from the floor with extreme attention to detail. Surveying my work with satisfaction, I told myself: "Here at least, then, my labor has not been in vain."

My next step was to search for the animal that had caused so much misery; I had finally made a firm decision to kill it. If I had been able to find it at that moment, there would have been no question about what would happen to it; but it seemed that the cunning creature had been frightened by my earlier violent rage, and chose not to show itself while I was in this state of mind. It's impossible to describe or even imagine the deep, wonderful sense of relief that the absence of this hated animal brought to my heart. It didn't appear during the night; and so for one night at least, since it had been brought into the house, I slept deeply and peacefully; yes, I slept even with the weight of murder on my conscience!

The second and third days went by, and my tormentor still hadn't appeared. Once more, I could breathe like a free man. The creature had fled the house forever in fear! I would never see it again! My joy was overwhelming! The guilt from my terrible act barely bothered me. A few questions had been asked, but I had easily answered them. They had even conducted a search—but naturally, nothing could be found. I considered my future happiness guaranteed.

On the fourth day after the murder, a group of police officers arrived at the house completely without warning and began conducting another thorough search of the property. However, confident in the perfect secrecy of my hiding place, I felt no anxiety at all. The officers asked me to join them during their investigation. They examined every single corner and crevice. Eventually, for the third or fourth time, they went down into the cellar. I didn't tremble even slightly. My heart beat as steadily as someone sleeping peacefully with a clear conscience. I walked back and forth across the entire cellar. I crossed my arms over my chest and moved around casually. The police were completely satisfied and got ready to leave. The joy in my heart was too overwhelming to contain. I felt compelled to say just one thing as a victory statement, something that would make them absolutely certain of my innocence.

"Gentlemen," I finally said as the group climbed the stairs, "I'm delighted to have put your suspicions to rest. I wish you all good health, and perhaps a bit more politeness. By the way, gentlemen, this—this is a very well-built house." (In my desperate need to say something casually, I barely knew what words were coming out of my mouth.)—"I can honestly say it's an excellently well-built house. These walls—are you leaving, gentlemen?—these walls are solidly constructed;" and here, driven by pure reckless boldness, I struck hard with a walking stick I was holding directly on that section of brickwork behind which lay the dead body of my beloved wife.

But may God protect and save me from the claws of the Devil! As soon as the echo of my strikes faded into silence, a voice from inside the tomb answered me!—a cry that began muffled and fragmented, like a child's weeping, then rapidly grew into one long, loud, and unending scream, completely unnatural and inhuman—a howl—a wailing shriek that was half terror and half victory, the kind that could only emerge from hell itself, rising together from the throats of the damned in their torment and the demons who rejoice in their destruction.

It would be pointless to describe my own thoughts at that moment. Feeling faint, I stumbled backward against the opposite wall. For a brief moment, the group on the stairs stood completely still, paralyzed by extreme terror and shock. The next instant, a dozen strong arms were working frantically at the wall. It collapsed entirely. The corpse, already severely decomposed and covered with dried blood, stood upright before the horrified onlookers. On its head, with its red gaping mouth and single glowing eye, perched the terrible creature whose cunning had led me to commit murder, and whose betraying cry had sealed my fate with the executioner. I had sealed the monster inside the tomb with me!

THE END

Thank You For Reading

You've Just Read a Piece of the Greatest Library Ever Rebuilt

Thank you for reading.

This book is one of thousands we're restoring, reimagining, and translating as part of the **Modern Library of Alexandria** — a global movement to preserve and share humanity's most important ideas.

What was once lost to fire and time is now rising again — not just as memory, but as living, breathing knowledge, freely accessible to all.

What You Can Do Next:

* **Keep Reading.**

   Discover more legendary works — in beautiful print, audiobook, or digital form — at LibraryofAlexandria.com.

* **Build Your Own Library.**

   Every title is available as a paperback, hardcover, or collectible boxset — at true printing cost. Craft a personal library worthy of display.

* **Spread the Light.**

   Share this book. Tell others about the movement. Help us translate every timeless work into every language, so no reader is ever left behind.

By finishing this book, you've already taken part in something extraordinary.

Join us at LibraryofAlexandria.com

Together, we're rebuilding the greatest library the world has ever known.

With appreciation,

The Modern Library of Alexandria Team

Visit:
www.libraryofalexandria.com
Or scan the code below:

www.ingramcontent.com/pod-product-compliance
Lightning Source LLC
Chambersburg PA
CBHW012206030726
47494CB00022B/2373